GW00859027

Nelson

English

Beginning Fiction Skills

RED
LEVEL

John Jackman   Wendy Wren

Little Bean

Everything I need.
Well, I need . . .

. . . my swimsuit,

my bucket and
spade, teddy,

Phil the Frog . . .

my crayons,

my rake, brush
and ball,

building blocks, a bowl,

my slide,

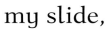

paddling pool,

and these . . .

Little Bean, don't be silly!
You can't take all of this!

But you said . . .
. . . EVERYTHING I need.

Well, I won't go on holiday then.

We'll have our own holiday, here in the shed.

Duncan's Tree House

On his birthday, Duncan's parents gave him a tree house.

Duncan's father was a builder. He had made the tree house in his workshop and he had fixed it to the tree the night before Duncan's birthday, when Duncan was asleep.

It was a complete surprise to Duncan.

Inside the tree house was a camp bed and a rug and a
table and a chair and a shelf with cups and plates on it.
There was a bookcase and a tin box for keeping things in.
The window had real glass in it, and opened and shut.

Duncan leaned out of the window and waved to his parents in the garden below.

"Thank you!" yelled Duncan.

8

"I'll put up a sign so that everyone will know whose house
it is," said Duncan.

He carved DUNCAN'S TREE HOUSE with his penknife
on a piece of wood, and painted it.

Then he nailed it to the hand rail outside his front door.

unit 3

Food Poems

Jelly on the Plate

Jelly on the plate,
Jelly on the plate,
Wibble, wobble,
Wibble, wobble,
Jelly on the plate.

The Pancake

Mix a pancake,
Stir a pancake,
    Pop it in the pan;

Fry the pancake,
Toss the pancake,
    Catch it if you can.

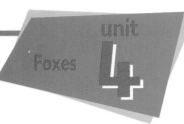

The Gingerbread Man

An old woman made a gingerbread man.
She opened the oven door.
He jumped out and ran away.

"Stop!" said the old woman.
But he did not stop.
He ran and ran.

A boy said, "Stop!"
A girl said, "Stop!"
But he did not stop.
He ran and ran.

A cat said, "Stop!"
A dog said, "Stop!"
But he did not stop.
He ran and ran.

The gingerbread man came to a river.

"I must cross the river," he said.

"I will help you cross the river," said the fox.

"Stand on my tail," said the fox.

"Stand on my back," said the fox.

"Stand on my nose," said the fox.

Jack and the Beanstalk

SCENE 1

A small garden where nothing is growing

MOTHER: Jack! Jack! Where are you?

JACK: Here I am!

MOTHER: Jack, we have no food to eat.
You will have to take the cow and
sell her.

JACK: Sell Daisy the cow!

MOTHER: I don't want to, but we need food.

Jack leads Daisy the cow out of the garden.

SCENE 2
On the road to the market

JACK: Come on, Daisy. Mother says I've got to sell you so we can buy food.

An old man steps out into the middle of the road.

OLD MAN: Where are you going with that cow?

JACK: I have to sell the cow so we can buy some food.

OLD MAN: You give me the cow. I will give you some magic beans in return.

JACK: What will I do with the beans?

OLD MAN: Plant them and you will see.

Jack gives the old man the cow and takes the beans.

18

SCENE 3

Jack's house

JACK: Mother! Mother! Where are you?

MOTHER: Here I am.

JACK: Look! I gave the cow to an old man and he gave me some magic beans.

Mother looks very cross. She throws the beans out of the window.

MOTHER: Beans! We needed money to get food! Go to bed! Go to bed with nothing to eat!

Mother sits down with her head in her hands.

          What are we going to do now?

Teddy Bear

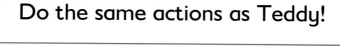

Do the same actions as Teddy!

Teddy bear,
Teddy bear, touch your nose,
Teddy bear,
Teddy bear, touch your toes,
Teddy bear,
Teddy bear, touch the ground,
Teddy bear,
Teddy bear, turn around.

Teddy bear,
Teddy bear, climb the stairs,
Teddy bear,
Teddy bear, say your prayers,
Teddy bear,
Teddy bear, turn off the light,
Teddy bear,
Teddy bear, say good night!

A Strange House

Hansel and Gretel were the children
of a poor woodman and his wife.
The woodman and his wife had no
money to buy food for the children.
One day, they took the children into
a dark wood and left them there.

The children looked around.
The wood was very big.
The wood was very dark.
They were frightened.

They walked through the dark, frightening wood.
They wanted to find their way home.

They walked and walked but they did not find their way home.
They found a little hut in the wood.

The walls of the hut were made of bread.

The roof of the hut was made of cake.

The windows of the hut were made of sweets.

Hansel took some of the wall to eat.

Gretel took some of the window to eat.

The door opened and an old woman came out.
Hansel and Gretel were frightened.
What should they do?

Mr Tig the Tiger

Bimla had to tidy her room because her cousin,
Satia, was coming to stay for the weekend.

Dad was cross that the room was in such a mess.
Bimla could not go out to play until all the toys
were put away and everything was neat and tidy.

She began to pick up the books and put them on the shelf. Dad came into the room carrying a black bin bag.

"Good girl," he said. "It won't take you very long."

"What's the bin bag for?" asked Bimla.

"I thought you could throw away some of the very old things."

"Why?" asked Bimla.

"Well," said Dad, "you have too much stuff in here and some of it is very old."

Bimla didn't think that was a very good idea.
She didn't want to throw things away.

"If I put a few things in the bag then Dad will
be pleased," she thought.

She looked round at the heap of toys. One of the
colouring books was ripped so she put it in the bag.
There was a jigsaw with pieces missing so she put
that in the bag.

Mr Tig, the old tiger, had an ear missing and the stuffing coming out of his leg.

"I will throw Mr Tig away," said Bimla.
She picked up the old tiger and put him in the bag.

"Don't throw me away!" said Mr Tig.

Bimla jumped. "Who said that?" she cried.

"Me," said the tiger from inside the bag. "I don't want to be thrown away!"

Bimla opened the bag and took out the old tiger.

"You can talk!" she said.

"Of course I can talk," said Mr Tig. "I can do lots of other things as well!"

After a Bath

After my bath
I try, try, try
to wipe myself
till I'm dry, dry, dry.

Hands to wipe
and fingers and toes
and two wet legs
and a shiny nose.

Just think how much
less time I'd take
if I were a dog
and could shake, shake, shake.